MW01610795

# Table of Contents

The follow book is reproduced below with the goal of providing information that is as accurate and reliable as possible. Regardless, purchasing this eBook can be seen as consent to the fact that both the publisher and the author of this book are in no way experts on the topics discussed within and that any recommendations or suggestions that are made herein are for entertainment purposes only. Professionals should be consulted as needed prior to undertaking any of the action endorsed herein.

This declaration is deemed fair and valid by both the American Bar Association and the Committee of Publishers Association and is legally binding throughout the United States.

Furthermore, the transmission, duplication or reproduction of any of the following work including specific information will be considered an illegal act irrespective of if it is done electronically or in print. This extends to creating a secondary or tertiary copy of the work or a recorded copy and is only allowed with express written consent from the Publisher. All additional right reserved.

The information in the following pages is broadly considered to be a truthful and accurate account of facts and as such any inattention, use or misuse of the information in question by the reader will render any resulting actions solely under their purview. There are no scenarios in which the publisher or the original author of this work can be in any fashion deemed liable for any hardship or damages that may befall them after undertaking information described herein.

Additionally, the information in the following pages is intended only for informational purposes and should thus be thought of as universal. As befitting its nature, it is presented without assurance regarding its prolonged validity or interim quality. Trademarks that are mentioned are done without written consent and can in no way be considered an endorsement from the trademark holder.

# Introduction

Do you often walk out of the kitchen and leave food on the stove? Perhaps you wonder why your pot roast is so dry when you have used a slow cooker? Maybe you just have a busy lifestyle, where you need to drop children from one activity to the next, with never enough time to make a meal? The instant pot is the answer to all your troubles.

You don't need a lot of time to create a proper dinner. You don't have to worry the meal will turn out too tough or dry because it was overcooked. The instant pot allows you to cook meals based on already tested time tables. The cooking details for chicken, beef, and other ingredients that are included with your instant pot will tell you the exact length of time to cook everything.

The guessing will be taken out of the cooking experience, so you have a quickly prepared meal that is tasty every time.

The details included in this guide are to help you with your new instant pot, the cooking process, why you want to use it versus a slow cooker or pressure cooker, and recipes to get you started.

Note that many of the recipes included in this guide can be adjusted for the number of people you are going to serve, whether it is yourself or a large party. The sections are designed to make it easier for you to find recipes based on your needs.

You will have at least five meals you can make for breakfast, lunch, and dinner. You also have access to special occasion meals that are great for certain holidays, and family gatherings.

The instant pot might be newer on the market and you may have a lot of questions right now, but at the end of this guide your questions will be answered. You will feel comfortable with, which pot to buy and how to use the pot you may already have to make great, quick meals.

Don't worry about the cooking anymore. Take charge of your routine, save time in the kitchen, and start eating better.

You can avoid those fast food drive thru and over salty meals at sit-down restaurants. You now have all you need to ensure proper nutrients are given to your body. You can stop feeling fatigue from too many carbs, feel full from a healthy meal, and know you are losing weight because you are stopping the salt, fat, and oil.

# Chapter 1: What is an Instant Pot

Plenty of terms are floating around the internet. It is like each time something new comes out there must be at least ten different names given to it, even something old that has been revamped for the new millennium can have a dozen different names. So, what does this have to do with "instant pot?" If you are like the author, then you may not know the difference between a Dutch oven, pressure cooker and crockpot. You might even think an instant pot is the same thing as at least one of the named kitchen appliances.

The thing is the hype and advertising make it a little confusing for those of us who don't cook a lot or have the time to keep up with every new kitchen appliance. For those of us who have busy lives, we just want to know there is a way to cook a great meal a little faster, such as a pot roast.

Yet, we will always ask the question of what appliance do we want? Can I buy this brand versus another?

To answer the question—what is an instant pot, you need to know that Instant Pot is a copyrighted, patented device. It is in fact what is known as an electric pressure cooker.

Yes, it is a glorified pressure cooker with a specific brand. There are different models available, which will be explored later. What you care about right now is understanding what makes it cook your meals quickly.

Sure, if you watch infomercials you know there are other electric cookers that promise to give you a full meal, faster than an oven, and at a reduced energy usage, like the NuWave. Yet, such a device uses infrared heat. Is it safe? Since it is not something we are going to debate, I won't answer that question. Instead, I'll tell you that the Instant Pot does not work using infrared heat. It uses electricity like any other electric kitchen appliance.

The reason it is better than historic pressure cookers is because you don't need the stove and it has a lot of predetermined settings to help you cook your meal quickly and to perfection.

## The Original Pressure Cooker

The original pressure cooker used the stove. The stove would heat up water in the bottom of the pot to increase the pressure inside a closed container. Steam would not be allowed to escape the lidded pot, but rather build up helping to soften the meat and veggies inside. The pressure also allowed a higher temperature to be reached inside the pot before the liquid would boil.

Denis Papin was the inventor of the pressure cooker in 1679. It was not until World War II that the idea took off because of fuel needs and time saving needs.

In 1991 the first patent was entered for the electric pressure cooker. It was designed to have more control over the process to ensure the perfect meal in as little time as possible.

The electric pressure cooker has several parts that all work to keep the pressure from building to an explosive point, while cooking the food inside. The drawback to the original pressure cooker was that it could reach too high a pressure and the lid would explode off the pot, making a mess of dinner. It took proper regulation and watching the pot to ensure your dinner turned out perfect.

All the guess work is no longer an issue. When you purchase a pressure cooker it will come with a lid that has a steam release, front valve, and external value. There is also a steam release that will release pressure if there is too much pressure build up in the bottom. It stops the lid from exploding off the top.

A sealing ring and anti-block shield are the next layer of protection. You have an inner pot where all the food is placed and an external pot. The external pot has all the controls and contains the base heating unit.

The design is to keep the outside cool so the counter does not melt underneath, while the internal temperature cooks the perfect meal. The control panel offers multiple choices from high pressure to low pressure, sauté, and stem features. You can also buy the appliance with a steam basket and trivet to help you cook various dishes.

The Instant Pot has all the above parts as described, but is the newest generation of pressure cookers available. You have access to some of the best technology in the kitchen that money can buy to make your family or yourself the perfect meal each time. All that is left is deciding how many functions you want your unit to have.

## How the Instant Pot Works?

The inner pot is either aluminum or stainless steel. Most aluminum inside pots are buffed or anodized. They are light weight and not dishwasher safe. The stainless-steel interior pot is three-ply or copper-clad on the bottom. These sturdier pots provide a uniformed heat.

Most Instant Pot pressure cookers are 3 quarts or 6.3 quart containers. Anything larger will make it difficult to maintain the pressure and it reduces the affordability of the Instant Pot.

The lid lock keeps the cooker in the sealed position. It is also what keeps the inner pot air-tight. It is important that the valves are in good condition and the inner ring is maintained to keep the pressure up and avoid issues. There are safety valves including a float valve to keep the pressure regulated.

The housing or heating unit has a temperature sensor, flat flexible board, and pressure sensor. When the heating is on the flexible board moves, but recovers at lower pressure. The pressure sensor will keep the pressure lower than working pressure. The process will keep going in a cycle with pressure lowing and the heating element cooling when the cooking is done.

Electric pressure cookers operate in a pressure range of 70 to 80 kilopascals, which is about 10.15 to 11.6 psi or pound-force per square inch. The internal temperature ranges between 239 degrees F and 244 degrees F. The heat and pressure will change based on the weight of the food. The different weights have preset heating durations.

It is the high pressure contained inside the pot combined with the steam from the water that helps make the food tender and cooked through.

# Chapter 2:  Why Choose Instant Pot?

The Instant Pot is a multifunctional cooker with various programmable settings. It has a manual and automatic mode. There are a couple of different versions of the Instant Pot, with the most recent one being the IP-DUO. It offers seven appliances, all in one. It is a slow cooker, pressure cooker, rice cooker, steam, sauté pan, yogurt maker, and a serving pot.

The Instant Pot offers 8 to 12 automatic function keys that have the most common cooking tasks preset for you. These preset settings help you push one button and start your meal without worry. These buttons include:

- Rice

- Porridge

- Sauté

- Soup

- Poultry

- Meat

- Stew

- Beans and chili

- Steaming

- Keep warm

- Slow cook

- Yogurt

You also have a delay button to set the time up to 24 hours, as well as the convenience of reducing the cooking time on meals up to 70% from a slow cooker or stove meal. The manual settings on the Instant Pot allow you to use your own recipes and timing to get the results you want. The programmed buttons are designed to offer you consistent results. For example, if you select rice it is preset to the 20-minute cooking time with at least 5 minutes to sit before you would fluff and serve.

The Instant Pot is going to help you delay cooking a meal, yet keep the food from spoiling. Let's say you want to prepare a meal before you leave the house, but don't want it to cook until you are closer to coming home. You can delay the cooking up to 24 hours.

An Instant Pot is designed to preserve the nutrients contained in the food you are going to eat. Medical studies have shown that slow cooking food tends to allow the nutrients to "leak" out of the food and dissipate before you eat. With a quicker cooking process the nutrients remain in the food, so you can benefit.

When you use one appliance for cooking, and it is a contained unit, your kitchen is going to be cleaner and offer a pleasanter cooking experience. It is easy for splatter from frying bacon or meat to get all around your kitchen when using a stove. You are saved from this when you have a lid on the items being cooked. More so, you are protected from making a mess in more than one pot. With the Instant Pot, you cook veggies, meat, and rice all together without worry. You will find your kitchen is less cluttered, there are no messy spills, and you no longer need to feel overwhelmed in the kitchen when making a meal.

## Energy Efficiency

The Instant Pot was designed to be a green appliance. It can help save up to 70% of the electricity you normally use when cooking on the stove top or in the oven. It is also going to save more energy than other comparable appliances, per the research. Less energy is consumed because of the quick cooking. The exterior of the pot is also well insulated with two layers to help keep the inner pot warm during operation. The operation of the Instant Pot also requires the heating element to be on only 40% of the cooking time. It turns on to maintain the temperature rather than remaining on the entire time. You also use less water for cooking since the pot is fully sealed. Not only is it energy efficient, it offers water conservation too.

## Safety Features

When discussing how the Instant Pot works, you learned it has built in safety features. These features are also a benefit and a reason to have an

Instant Pot. The original pressure cooker had a lot of issues with safety, mostly attributed to user error. However, it also had a great deal to do with how the pot was made. The Instant Pot has improved upon the safety and earned the UL/ULC certification. There are 10 safety features:

1.  Lid close detection – this feature will tell you if the lid is not properly closed and not allow operation at high pressures.

2.  Leaky lid protection – in the event the seal ring is missing or not in proper working order the pot will let you know.

3.  Lid lock under pressure- the lid will always lock when in use.

4.  Anti-blockage vent – the steam release vent has a shield to prevent jamming by food.

5.  Automatic temperature control – the thermostat regulates the temperature within a safe zone to eliminate accidents.

6.  High temperature warning – this is a warning sound that tells you if the pressure is too high. The pot will stop heating at specific limits.

7.  Automatic pressure control – there is a sensor that maintains a proper psi inside the pot.

8.  Extreme temperature and power protection – the pot has a power disconnect should temperatures reach higher than the set limit of 336 degrees F. It will also turn off if there is a high electrical current that draws on the cooker. It prevents an unsafe situation during a power surge or other electrical issue.

9.  Excess pressure protection – the pressure regulator may malfunction, which is why there is an internal mechanism that will release steam if pressure builds too high.

10. Pressure regulator protection – again this has to do with releasing pressure, in this case steam to decrease the pressure in the pot.

These features protect you, but also make the Instant Pot more beneficial to your cooking needs than other pressure cooking pots on the market.

# Chapter 3: How to Choose an Instant Pot that Is Good

There are different versions of the Instant Pot on the market. The newest version is the IP DUO with 7 in 1 functions. Instant Pot also released a 6-in-1 IP-LUX50, IP Bluetooth version, IP-DUO60 stainless steel version, IP-DUO 6-in-1 stainless steel version, and two different sizes.

First when talking about choosing an Instant Pot, you need to realize that it is a proprietary product. Instant Pot is a type of pressure cooker. It could be compared to the Cuisinart CPC-600 6 quarts 1000-watt electric pressure cooker. It can also be compared to its other versions as listed in the above paragraph.

There are a few things you need to decide for yourself when it comes to buying an Instant Pot versus a different electric pressure cooker, as well as which Instant Pot model you want.

It is due diligence to compare other electric pressure cooker models. They will not be compared here for you. This chapter will assume that you are going to choose an Instant Pot and the question is what model you want.

## Next Gen

Companies use their R&D departments to research and develop new products, fixing old issues and improving upon other functions. For the very reason that Instant Pot wishes you to have a pressure cooker that fits your lifestyle, they offer different versions including their next generation products.

Currently, the newest model is their 7-in-1 multifunction pressure cooker. However, you can also shop around for earlier models like the 6-in-1 electric pressure cooker. If you are a person that needs to have the latest technology—always, then you are going to want the newest model on the market.

If you are looking for inexpensive and functional, you may sacrifice certain features to find a more cost effective Instant Pot model for your needs.

## Size

More than next generation appliances, you should concern yourself with the size of the device. Are you a single person? Do you have a family gathering of ten or more people? The amount of cooking you are going to do inside of your Instant Pot matters. You may need the 6-quart Instant Pot to ensure you have enough internal cooking space for the large meals you will make on a daily basis. For a single person who rarely entertains, a 3-quart pressure cooker is more than enough.

## Stainless Steel or Aluminum

Aluminum is the cheaper material. It is also lighter and easier to dent if you drop the pot accidentally. Aluminum is a good option if you must watch your pennies. If you can afford it, you want the stainless-steel construction.

## Bluetooth Functions

Are you planning on making meals in the pot while you are not home? If you intend on preparing the food and leaving the house, then you might wish to have the Bluetooth function and the delay function. First, the Bluetooth will work when the pot is in range, which means you could be in the garage or outside and potentially start the cooking process. It is not a long-distance feature, but you could be getting ready for work and know you need to start the pot. With Bluetooth connectivity, you should be able to make that happen. The delay function also helps you start the pot when you are not near it. You must have the ingredients prepared, of course, but at least you know the pot will start cooking and have a hot meal ready when you arrive home.

## How Many Functions

How many functions do you want to have automatically stored in your pot? The IP-DUO is sold as a 7-in-1, where there are 12 preset options. You are going to pay a little more for this advanced technology, so ask yourself is it worth it? Is the extra cost negligible and will you use all 7 functions? Sometimes saving $5 can be more important to you than one extra function or presets.

These are just some of the concepts you should consider when you choose an Instant Pot that will work. When you start the shopping process, you must pay attention to which pot is being sold. There are three online stores that sell Instant Pots:

- Instant Pot Online Store

- Amazon

- Walmart

There are also brick and mortar based stores, but they are all based in Canada. The online stores will sell two versions of the same Instant Pot. One version is US measurement based, meaning the temperature is all in Fahrenheit. There are also International versions that use the metric and Celsius units of measurement. Most of the pots are going to come with English, Spanish, Chinese, and French instructions and recipes too, as a way to help multiple customers purchase the same product.

As you shop around to check prices, look at Instant Pot's website. They offer additional options such as Instant Pot yogurt cups, the steam rack and mini mitts to help carry the interior pot. You will want to have the accessories that make the most sense based on what you are going to be cooking.

**Note: Instant Pot's online store does list one product with an 8-quart pot. However, the statement that 6-quarts is the biggest you want to go is still true. For an even cooking process, with proper pressure, tests show 6-quarts is the best size for large meals.**

# Chapter 4: Do's and Don'ts of Instant Pots

Instant Pot is a great appliance to have, but there are still some safe operating procedures, as well as handy little suggestions that can make your experience even better. To help you decide if the Instant Pot is for you and help you with the recipes you are going to find in here, you definitely need to understand the do's and don'ts of using the Instant Pot.

## It is not Intuitive

The Instant Pot is not going to replace your thought process. The Instant Pot does require you to get use to how it works, unlike a slow cooker that you put food in and walk away from in about five minutes. Yes, there are preset cooking times; however, these are standard for the majority of people—not specific to you. You may need to use manual modes to cook a steak at medium rare versus well-done.

The best thing you can do is keep your recipes simple for the first few times you use the Instant Pot. Discover how to cook eggs, beans, or vegetables before going to a full course meal all in the same pot.

Think of your Instant Pot like a new oven. Your old oven had some quirks. It stopped working properly, but you learned to deal with its idiosyncrasies. For example, the back of the heating element may have cooked your food a little faster, so you had to rotate your baking sheet to ensure you didn't burn the back row of food and undercook the front. You also learned that your oven was better at operating at 325 degrees F for cookies versus 350 degrees F. Your instant pot will require you to get to know it. It won't have uneven cooking, but it will need some adjustment based on what you like and how you like to eat the food you make.

## Cleaning

When you clean your Instant Pot, you will only want to wipe down the outer surface. Never expose the exterior pot to water submersion. When you clean the inside of the exterior pot, use a damp rag, not a dripping rag, to remove any hair or other particles that have fallen in.

The cleaning process is easy, which also makes the Instant Pot friendlier than other options on the market. The interior pot should be hand-washed along with the sealing ring and lid. This will protect it for years to come. Yes, stainless-steel may be "dishwasher" safe, according to the instructions, but over time it can deteriorate or become spotted or pitted. Save yourself from needing to purchase a new interior pot by handwashing it. One pot, the ring, and lid is not a huge amount of dishes to clean, and handwashing it will keep you happily eating Instant Pot meals for years.

**Converting Recipes for the Instant Pot**

Some of the recipes you may come across as you begin to use your Instant Pot more and more, will be for other types of pressure cookers. The timing of these recipes will need to be adjusted. Most pressure cookers operate at 15psi. Since the Instant Pot works at 11.6psi, you will need to add a few minutes to the other pressure cooker recipes you come across. It will be an adjustment period, where you check if the food is done and add more time, when necessary.

**Canning with your Pressure Pot?**

One of the most popular questions about the Instant Pot is whether you can use it to can, since it builds pressure inside. You would think it would seal containers, but it is not a canning device. It does not offer that function. DO NOT use the Instant Pot for canning. First, the USDA has not approved the Instant Pot for canning because it has not tested it for safety in canning. Secondly, the company does not include this function in their 7-in-1 function, so do not put yourself in a dangerous situation by trying to can with your new electric pressure cooker.

**Add a Second Stainless Steel Insert**

It might seem like you are being sold the Instant Pot and its accessories. This is not the intention, but to point out that you have options. There are reasons to have the accessories, such as the yogurt cups. First, you know they are approved to go in the Instant Pot and second, you can make yogurt at home if you like to eat it. It is fun and saves you money at the store.

Mentioning the purchase of a second insert is for preference purposes. Let's say you need to make a meal to feed 20 people, but 6-quarts will not provide you with enough space. With a second insert you can make the meal twice and feed everyone who is visiting your home. It is also nice to have a second insert for those nights when you don't want to wash the insert. You might decide you want to store the pot in the fridge with leftovers and need to cook a new meal in the morning.

The point is you can gain a little extra time from cleaning your insert if you have more than one.

These are just a few of the do's and don'ts that will make operating your Instant Pot a little easier and keep it around for years. Always read the instructions of your new pot and double check the recipes you are going to use to ensure that you are making a proper meal, within the safety of the devices "usage." Enjoy getting used to your new Instant Pot and the meals like the following recipes that you can have.

# Chapter 5: Breakfast Recipes

Breakfast is considered the most important meal of the day, and it should be. This is the meal that will get you through the morning, provide you energy, and tell your body how it should feel for the day. If you lack nutrients at breakfast or amp up on coffee with no food, then your body is not going to feel its best. It will be sluggish. The recipes in this section are aimed at providing enough protein and vitamins, so you can tackle whatever you need to for the day.

**Quinoa with Fresh Fruit**

Quinoa can be a great replacement for anyone who loves oatmeal or wants to try a warm cereal that is not oatmeal. It is considered healthier than many breakfast options, and offers a high fiber meal. You can dress up quinoa in several ways to make it different each day you wish to have a hot meal.

SERVES: Six

PREPARATION TIME: about 20 minutes

INGREDIENTS:

- 1 ½ cups quinoa, uncooked and rinsed

- 2 ¼ cups water

- ½ teaspoon vanilla

- 2 tablespoons maple syrup

- ¼ teaspoon cinnamon, ground

- Optional: fresh berries, milk, sliced almonds

INSTRUCTIONS:

1. Place the quinoa, water, vanilla, syrup, cinnamon, and a touch of salt in your instant pot.

2. Select high pressure, cook one minute.

3. Turn your instant pot off, let stand for 10 minutes.

4. Use the quick pressure release to make sure all the pressure has been released.

5. Remove the lid carefully to avoid steam issues.

6. Fluff the quinoa.

7. Serve with milk, berries, and sliced almonds if desired.

ADDITIONAL SUGGESTIONS:

Consider adding a little brown sugar instead of maple syrup.

## Yogurt

Yogurt is going to be a breakfast item you prepare the night before or the day before. It does have the longest cooking time of any recipe in this book, but yogurt is also a very healthy meal that can be added to granola, eaten with berries, and help you gain probiotics you need to stay healthy. You can store the yogurt for two weeks. Also, the longer you leave the yogurt in your instant pot the tarter it will be, so you may wish to adjust the time to fit your tastes.

SERVES: Four

PREPARATION TIME: about 8 hours and 20 minutes

INGREDIENTS:

- 4 teaspoons yogurt with live culture

- 32 ounces of milk

- 1 cup water

INSTRUCTIONS:

1. You will need the small size mason jars (8 ounces).

2. Pour the water into the cooker.

3. Use a steamer rack, placing it in position.

4. Fill the jars with the milk, about 8 ounces each.

5. Place the jars inside the cooker and put it on steam.

6. Steam for one minute.

7. Let the instant pot cool down.

8. The milk needs to reach 115 degrees F.

9. Remove the jars.

10. Add 1 teaspoon live culture into each jar.

11. Place the jars in the instant pot again, this time programming it for 8 hours.

ADDITIONAL SUGGESTIONS:

When you are ready to eat your yogurt, add fresh fruit to the bowl. Granola is also a helpful addition, for the fiber, as well as the full feeling you need to have after eating breakfast.

## Korean Eggs and Rice

This is a recipe that will use certain "Asian" ingredients, which can make it a Korean style egg or simply an Asian egg. It is served over rice, and can include vegetables if you wish to add more vitamins and minerals to your breakfast meal.

SERVES: One

PREPARATION TIME: 30 minutes

INGREDIENTS:

- 1 cup rice

- 1 cup water for the rice

- 1 large egg

- Chopped scallions

- 1/3 cups cold water

- Sesame seeds

- Garlic powder

- Salt

- Pepper

INSTRUCTIONS:

1. Use a rice cooker.

2. Combine 1 cup each of water and rice.

3. Set the rice cooker to cook the rice.

4. After 20 minutes, start the egg part of your meal.

5. Scramble the egg in a bowl with the water.

6. Strain the egg mixture over a mesh strainer into a heat proof bowl.

7. Mix in the sesame seeds, garlic powder, salt, and pepper to taste.

8. Place the steamer basket inside your instant pot.

9. Put the egg mixture in the bowl, in the steamer basket.

10. Cover the lid, set to high, with a timer of 5 minutes.

11. Serve immediately.

ADDITIONAL SUGGESTIONS:

Consider adding in vegetables, such as peppers, onions, bean sprouts, carrots, and other veggies you typically see in Asian dishes.

## Eggs de Provence

Eggs de Provence is one of the most popular Sunday breakfast ideas that you could have any morning of the week, when you use an Instant Pot. You can get the mixture started and prepare for your day while your breakfast cooks.

SERVES: Six

PREPARATION TIME: about 40 minutes

INGREDIENTS:

- 6 eggs

- 1 cup ham or bacon, cooked

- 1 small onion, chopped

- 1 cup kale leaves, chopped

- ½ cup heavy cream

- 1 cup cheddar cheese

- 1 teaspoon herbs de Provence

- Salt and pepper to taste

INSTRUCTIONS:

1. Whisk the eggs with the heavy cream.

2. Add in the rest of the ingredients, until mixed well.

3. Pour the mixture into a heat proof dish.

4. Add a cup of water to the bottom of the instant pot.

5. Use a trivet or steamer basket.

6. Using manual settings, select high and cook 20 minutes.

7. Let sit for 10 minutes for the steam to escape.

8. Serve immediately.

## ADDITIONAL SUGGESTIONS:

If you do not keep herbs de Provence on hand, you can use the individual herbs from your spice storage. The mix contains savory, marjoram, thyme, rosemary, and oregano. Some mixes have lavender too. Serve with veggies or fruit, as well as an English muffin.

## Hardboiled Eggs

If you love eggs in a variety of ways, then you will enjoy making hard boiled eggs for a meal or two. Not only can they make a great breakfast, but you can chop them up for a salad you have for lunch.

SERVES: One or more

PREPARATION TIME: about 5 minutes

INGREDIENTS:

- Eggs

- 1 cup water

INSTRUCTIONS:

1. Get your steamer basket or trivet.

2. Add 1 cup of water to the instant pot and submerge the steamer basket.

3. Place as many eggs as you wish in the pot, up to one layer. Never stack the eggs.

4. Use the manual setting to select high pressure.

5. Cooking times are 5 minutes for hard boiled, 4 minutes for soft boiled, and 1 minute for poached eggs.

6. After the steam, quick releases, put the eggs in a bowl of cold water.

ADDITIONAL SUGGESTIONS:

You can garnish the eggs in any way you wish. You will want to keep the water cold to help you peel the eggs. It is best to peel them right after they are cool instead of waiting until you are ready to eat them. The longer they go unpeeled and cold, the harder it will be to peel them. Depending on the size of your instant pot you might be able to cook a dozen or 18 eggs for multiple breakfast meals, salads, or deviled eggs. Deviled eggs are great if you plan on having a brunch. The timing is also quicker since you don't have to wait for the water to boil. To make hard boiled eggs a complete breakfast, add bacon, an English muffin and fruit to your plate.

# Chapter 6: Lunch Recipes

It can be tough to fit lunch in during working hours, which is why you need to have something you can make at home quickly the night before or in the morning. Soups paired with salads are a great option because they are both light menu items, filled with protein and nutrients you need, without making you tired in the afternoon. Most of the recipes in this section are geared more towards keeping you up and awake after a meal versus sleep in the afternoon. We all know how easy it is to reach for another cup of coffee or want to take a nap because lunch was "too heavy."

**Beef and Vegetable Soup**

Beef and vegetable soup is a classic. It is perfect for those winter temperatures, when you want to warm up and stay warm all day.

SERVES: Eight

PREPARATION TIME: 1 ¼ hours

INGREDIENTS:

- 1-pound beef short ribs, boneless and trimmed, cut into ½ inch pieces

- 2 tablespoons vegetable oil

- 1 onion, finely chopped

- 2 teaspoons fresh thyme, minced

- 2 tablespoons tomato paste

- 1 garlic clove, minced

- 2 tablespoons all-purpose flour

- 6 cups beef broth

- ½ cup dry red wine

- 3 carrots, peeled, cut into ½ inch strips

- 1 pound red potatoes, cut into ¾ inch pieces

- 2 celery ribs, ½ inch in size

- 2 tablespoons fresh parsley (optional)

- 2 bay leaves

INSTRUCTIONS:

1. Season the beef with a little salt and pepper.

2. Set your instant pot to sauté, place the beef and a little oil in the bottom.

3. Brown the meat for 5 minutes, making sure all sides are browned.

4. Add the rest of the ingredients to the pot.

5. Set the instant pot for 15 minutes, based on the appropriate meat setting.

6. Let the pressure release for another 15 minutes

7.   Serve.

ADDITIONAL SUGGESTIONS:

You can also turn this into a beef and barley soup by omitting the potatoes and adding in ½ cup barley. You would need to let the barley simmer for 10 minutes before adding the rest of the ingredients to the pot.

**Turkey Breast and Gravy**

Turkey is a great lunch meal, especially, when sliced and served with gravy. Whether you are looking for a brunch option or something you can reheat during the week, this recipe can fulfill your wishes.

SERVES: Six

PREPARATION TIME: 1 ½ hours, approximately

INGREDIENTS:

- 1 6-pound turkey

- 2 tablespoons butter

- 1 onion, finely chopped

- 1 ½ teaspoon dried sage

- 1 carrot, peeled and chopped

- 1 garlic clove, peeled and smashed

- 3 tablespoons flour

- 2 cups chicken broth

- ¼ cup white wine

- 1 bay leaf

INSTRUCTIONS:

1. Melt the butter in your microwave and rub over the turkey, adding pepper and salt to taste.

2. Brown the turkey for 5 minutes in the instant pot using the sauté function.

3. Add in the onion and carrot for five minutes.

4. Add the garlic, sautéing it for 30 seconds with the turkey, onion and carrots.

5. Remove the turkey.

6. Stir in the flour and cook for another minute.

7. Whisk in the wine, making sure to remove any lumps.

8. Add in the broth and bay leaf.

9. Place the turkey back in the instant pot.

10. Set the pot for high, until it reaches pressure.

11. Reduce to medium-high for 35 minutes.

12. Use the quick release pressure button.

13. Put the turkey on a carving board.

14. Let it rest for 15 minutes.

15. Meanwhile, bring the liquid to a boil to reduce the broth and make a gravy.

ADDITIONAL SUGGESTIONS:

You can add additional vegetables, such as potatoes to make a full meal.

**Mongolian Beef**

Mongolian beef can be made as spicy as you want it. It also makes a great light lunch on the weekends.

SERVES: Six

PREPARATION TIME: 30 minutes

INGREDIENTS:

- 3 cups rice

- 3 cups water for rice

- 2-pounds flank steak, cut into ¼ inch strips

- 1 tablespoon vegetable oil

- ½ cup soy sauce, lite salt

- 4 garlic cloves, minced or pressed

- ½ cup water

- ½ teaspoon ginger, fresh and minced

- 2/3 cup brown sugar

- 3 tablespoons water

- 3 green onions, 1 inch slices

INSTRUCTIONS:

1. Start by combining 3 cups of rice and 3 cups of water in a rice cooker, set to cook.

2. Season the beef with pepper to taste.

3. Put the oil in your pot and sauté the meat until brown on each side.

4. Remove the meat

5. Add the garlic to the pot and sauté for 1 minute.

6. Add the soy sauce, water, brown sugar, and ginger.

7. Stir to combine.

8. Put the beef back in the pot.

9. Set for high pressure for 12 minutes.

10. Use the quick release button to let the steam off.

ADDITIONAL SUGGESTIONS:

The rice will take longer to cook. It is 30 minutes in most rice cookers. The meat will take 20 minutes from prep to completion. Add in desired vegetables, such as carrots and broccoli when you put the meat back in the pot.

**Minestrone**

A great accompanying dish for pasta or the perfect lunch, minestrone provides protein from the beans and nutrients from the vegetables. It is also a quick soup you can make in the morning before work and reheat when you need it. 0

SERVES: Four

PREPARATION TIME: 18 minutes

INGREDIENTS:

- 2 tablespoons oil

- 1 large, diced, onion

- 2 celery stalks, diced

- 1 diced carrot

- 1 teaspoon oregano

- 3 minced garlic cloves

- 1 teaspoon basil

- 28-ounces fresh tomatoes

- 15-ounces white beans, drained and cooked

- 4 cups vegetable broth

- 1 cup pasta, elbow

- 1/3 cup grated Parmesan cheese

INSTRUCTIONS:

1. Set to sauté mode.

2. Place onions, oil, carrots, celery, and garlic in the pot.

3. Cook until soft.

4. Add in the oregano, salt and pepper to taste.

5. Dice the tomatoes.

6. Put the tomatoes, broth, basil and pasta in the instant pot.

7. Cook on high for 6 minutes.

8. When the timer goes off, let it stand for 2 minutes.

9. Vent the steam.

10. Add the kidney beans.

11. Garnish with Parmesan cheese.

12. Serve.

ADDITIONAL SUGGESTIONS:

Minestrone is great with a salad or crackers. The beans help provide protein. You can consider adding different kinds of beans to change the flavor, as well as enhance the amount of protein you are getting from this meal.

**Gumbo**

Gumbo is one of the most popular dishes from New Orleans. It contains a variety of healthy herbs and spices that can help provide immunity. You also have different protein options to put in the gumbo, such as chicken and smoked sausage.

SERVES: Six

PREPARATION TIME: 30 minutes of active preparation

INGREDIENTS:

- 1-pound chicken, boneless, skinless

- 1-pound pork sausage

- 1 tablespoon coconut oil

- 1 medium white onion

- 6 cups of tomatoes, chopped

- 3 green bell peppers, sliced

- 2 stalks celery

- 2 carrots

- 2 cups vegetable or chicken broth

- ¼ cup parsley

- 6 garlic cloves

- 1 teaspoon thyme

- ½ teaspoon red chili flakes

- ½ teaspoon paprika

- ¼ teaspoon black pepper

- ½ teaspoon cayenne

- 1 bay leaf

INSTRUCTIONS:

1. Heat the coconut oil in the instant pot.

2. Select sauté to brown the chicken and sausage.

3. Slice your vegetables while the meats are browning.

4. Remove the meat from the pot once browned.

5. Sauté the vegetables.

6. Mince the garlic and add it to the pan.

7. Add in the broth and tomatoes, bringing the mixture to a simmer.

8. Add in the chicken and sausage, after slicing it into small pieces.

9. Stir all ingredients in and make certain the mixture is evenly spiced.

10. Cook for 10 minutes.

11. Serve warm.

ADDITIONAL SUGGESTIONS:

If you are going to use fish or shellfish instead of sausage or chicken, it is important to note you will not need to sauté the fish, but will only need to cook it for a maximum of 5 minutes depending on the seafood used. If you cook the seafood too long it can become tough.

# Chapter 7: Dinner Recipes

Dinner or supper is a great time to have a family meal that is wholesome and nutritious. The dinner recipes in this section are designed for quick preparation and cooking time, but also to give you a great Sunday meal like pot roast. The recipes are main entrees and can be served with starches, veggies, and fruits to ensure a well-balanced meal is attained.

**Pot Roast**

Pot roast is a good wholesome meal. You will want to choose a cut of beef that has a little fat on it to help make it more tender within the cooking time. You will need to add preparation time for your meal the larger the pot roast is. This recipe is for approximately 3 pounds of meat, so consider 10 minutes of cooking time per additional pound.

SERVES: Four or more

PREPARATION TIME: 1 hour

INGREDIENTS:

- 1-pound chuck roast for each person

- ½ cup onion, chopped

- 1 to 2 garlic cloves, minced

- 1 teaspoon black pepper, fresh ground

- 2 cups water or enough to cover the roast in the instant pot

- One potato per person

- 3 to 4 strips of bacon

- ½ carrot for each person, diced or cut into rounds

INSTRUCTIONS:

1. Cut the roast in half

2. Place the onions, garlic, and pepper in the instant pot with the roast.

3. Use the sauté feature to brown the roast on each side.

4. Add in the rest of the ingredients.

5. Cover and seal the pot, setting the timer for meat and 35 minutes.

6. Let the pot vent after the cooking time has ended.

7. Remove the meat, break it into chunks.

8. Set the instant pot to sauté again for 10 minutes to reduce the water, add in a package of gravy mix or xanthan gum to make gravy.

9. Turn off the heat when you have the desired gravy consistency.

10. Plate the meat, with the vegetables and gravy.

ADDITIONAL SUGGESTIONS:

You can add in more vegetables or even a little balsamic vinegar to enhance the taste of your pot roast.

## Pork Vindaloo

Pork Vindaloo is an Indian dish that works great for weeknights. It cooks quickly and offers spices that help build immunity.

SERVES: Six

PREPARATION TIME: 1 ½ hours, approximately

INGREDIENTS:

- 3-pounds pork butt, trimmed and cut into 1 inch pieces

- 3 onions, finely chopped

- 2 tablespoons vegetable oil

- 8 garlic cloves, minced

- 1 tablespoon paprika

- 1 tablespoon mustard seeds

- 1 teaspoon ground cumin

- ¼ teaspoon cayenne pepper

- ¼ cup all-purpose flour

- 1/8 teaspoon ground cloves

- 2 fresh tomatoes, diced

- 1 cup chicken broth

- 1 teaspoon sugar

- ¼ cup cilantro, fresh and minced

INSTRUCTIONS:

1. Set your instant pot to sauté.

2. Use pepper and salt for seasoning on the pork.

3. Place your pork and 1 tablespoon of oil in the pot and brown the meat on all sides.

4. Browning the meat should take 8 minutes.

5. Remove the meat, use the other tablespoon to sauté the onions, mustard seeds, cumin, cayenne, cloves, and paprika. It takes 30 seconds.

6. Add in all ingredients except the pork to create a smooth seasoned liquid.

7. Place the meat in the pot.

8. Set for 30 minutes in the instant pot.

9. Let the pressure out naturally.

10. Plate and Serve.

ADDITIONAL SUGGESTIONS:

Pork Vindaloo is a great recipe to have with a side of rice. You can either cook the rice in the pot or use a rice cooker. You can also use lamb instead of pork, as it is a classic choice for the vindaloo recipe. Cinnamon, mace, or nutmeg can also be used as other spices if you do not like paprika or cumin.

**Fiesta Steak**

Fiesta Steak is a recipe filled with plenty of vegetables, thus lots of vitamin C. This is a great way to help your kids get some of the essential nutrients they need.

SERVES: Four

PREPARATION TIME: 1 hour

INGREDIENTS:

- 2 cups white or brown rice

- 2 cups water or broth

- 3 ounces of steak per person (approximately 1 pound of steak)

- 1 tablespoon cilantro

- ¼ cup fresh lime juice

- 1 teaspoon cumin, fresh and ground

- 1 tablespoon fresh oregano

- 4 minced garlic cloves

- 1 each: yellow, red, and green bell pepper, sliced into strips

- 1 onion, sliced into strips

INSTRUCTIONS:

1. Prep your instant pot.

2. Rinse the rice and drain.

3. Layer the bottom of your instant pot with the rice.

4. In a small bowl, mix your seasonings.

5. Add the seasonings to the water or broth.

6. Gently pour the water over the rice, if necessary layer it smooth again.

7. Set the steak gently over the rice.

8. Add the peppers and onions.

9. Cook for 35 minutes.

10. Check the steak for proper internal temperature.

11. Serve.

ADDITIONAL SUGGESTIONS:

Depending on the steak you may need more time. Some cuts are tougher than others. A New York strip should be tender already, so require less time than a bottom cut. Use fresh ingredients for a healthier meal.

**Chili**

Who doesn't love a good bowl of chili for an easy weeknight meal? The best part is that you can make chili in less than 30 minutes, when using an instant pot versus the 30 minutes to an hour you need on the stove.

SERVES: Four

PREPARATION TIME: approximately 45 minutes, 10 in the instant pot

INGREDIENTS:

- 1 onion, chopped

- 2 tablespoons vegetable oil

- 1-pound ground beef, as lean as possible

- 2 tablespoons chili powder

- 2 teaspoons ground cumin

- 4 minced garlic cloves

- 1 can crushed tomatoes

- 2 cans kidney beans, rinsed

- 1 cup chicken broth

INSTRUCTIONS:

1. Set your instant pot to sauté.

2. Add in the onions and 1 tablespoon oil into the pot.

3. Stir in the chili powder, garlic, cumin, and a little salt.

4. Cook for about 1 minute.

5. Add the beef and cook for 4 minutes.

6. Stir in the tomatoes and broth.

7. Set the instant pot for 10 minutes.

8. Use the quick release for the pressure.

9. Stir in the beans, set the instant pot to sauté to simmer the beans for 5 minutes.

10. Serve.

The preparation time and cook time are a total of 45 minutes, with about 20 to 25 minutes of cooking time to mix the flavors and avoid overcooking the beans.

ADDITIONAL SUGGESTIONS:

Serve with cornbread. You can start the cornbread first to ensure that both are ready at the same time.

## Meatloaf

Meatloaf is a meal that usually takes 1 ½ hours from start to finish, unless you have an instant pot. Meatloaf is an American staple that many families love because it is affordable, easy, and quick to make. It also reheats well and can be taken for lunch, when there are leftovers.

SERVES: Four

PREPARATION TIME: 45 minutes, with only 25 minutes under pressure

INGREDIENTS:

- ½ cup panko or other bread crumbs

- 2 ½ cups marinara sauce

- 1 ½ pounds ground beef

- 1-ounce Parmesan cheese

- ¼ cup basil

- 1 large egg, beaten

- ¼ teaspoon garlic, minced

- 6 slices provolone cheese

INSTRUCTIONS:

1. Follow your usual steps for combining the beef with the grated cheese, spices, egg, marinara sauce, and bread crumbs.

2. Form a loaf with the meat.

3. Place the loaf in the instant pot and cover with the remaining 2 cups marinara sauce.

4. Cook for 25 minutes.

5. Let the steam release.

6. Open the lid, cover the loaf with the provolone cheese.

7. Melt the cheese for 5 minutes.

8. Transfer the loaf to a cutting board.

9. Cut and serve the meatloaf.

ADDITIONAL SUGGESTIONS:

This is an Italian meatloaf recipe; however, you can decide to make a ketchup based meatloaf if you wish. Simply change the marinara sauce to ketchup, use American or cheddar cheese, and leave out the basil.

# Chapter 8: Special Occasion Recipes

Special occasions arise throughout your life, whether it is a wedding, christening, or holiday. The recipes in this section are all geared towards more important events in your family, whether it is a small gathering of your closest relatives or a friendly party.

**Kalua Pig Recipe**

Hawaii certainly knows how to provide a wonderful luau, with a perfectly cooked pig. Now, you can bring this taste home with you and cook it in an instant pot to ensure you get to enjoy it. This is great for special occasions, such as birthday parties, anniversaries, or promotions at work.

SERVES: Eight

PREPARATION TIME: 2 hours

INGREDIENTS:

- 3 slices bacon

- 5 peeled garlic cloves

- 5-pounds bone in pork, shoulder roast

- 1 tablespoon Hawaiian sea salt

- 1 cup water

- 1 cabbage, cored, cut it into 6 wedges

INSTRUCTIONS:

1. Put the bacon pieces in the bottom of your instant pot.

2. Press sauté for about a minute or until the bacon starts sizzling.

3. Cut the pork into 3 equal pieces.

4. Cut a couple of slits in each of the pork pieces.

5. Taking your garlic cloves, cut them into pieces and start stuffing the various slits you made with the pork.

6. Salt the pork, evenly.

7. Create one layer of pork on top of the bacon.

8. Add the water.

9. Set the timer for 90 minutes.

10. Let the instant pot release the steam.

11. Check to see if the meat is tender. If it is not cooked the roast for another 5 to 10 minutes.

12. Remove the pork.

13. Place the cabbage in the pot.

14. Replace the lid and cook the cabbage for 3 to 5 minutes.

15. Put the cabbage on your plate, Serve the pork on the bed of cabbage.

ADDITIONAL SUGGESTIONS:

You can adjust the seasonings you use, such as adding in a little pineapple juice and then cooking pineapple pieces for 2 to 3 minutes after you cook the cabbage. Use the water as a sauce by cooking it down and adding a little soy sauce to the pineapple flavored water.

**Turkey Breast**

Turkey is the perfect Thanksgiving or Christmas main entrée. When cooking it in an instant pot, it will take less time and produce a moister turkey for your entire family to enjoy.

SERVES: Four or more

PREPARATION TIME: 1 hour and 15 minutes, approximately

INGREDIENTS:

- Whole turkey or turkey breast

- Butter

- Salt

- Pepper

- 1 cup water

INSTRUCTIONS:

1. Thaw the turkey breast as you would on any holiday.

2. Make certain the turkey is the correct size to fit in your pot with the trivet. The size of the turkey determines how many it will feed.

3. Wash the turkey and remove the innards.

4. Place one cup of water in the bottom of the instant pot.

5. Cut slits in the turkey skin and insert butter, salt and pepper.

6. Place the turkey in the pot.

7. Set on manual time for 45 minutes.

8. Let the pressure slowly release for an additional 20 minutes.

9. Check the temperature to make certain it is 180 to 190 degrees F.

10. Serve.

## ADDITIONAL SUGGESTIONS:

Since the turkey will take at least 1 hour and 15 minutes from prep to the table, you have plenty of time to make side dishes to go along with your turkey. Perhaps you will cook some potatoes, mash them, and make gravy from the water from the instant pot. Also, consider having a type of bread, fruit, and green bean casserole with your turkey dinner.

**Warmed Ham with Brown Sugar Glazing**

Ham is another special occasion staple. Any ham you obtain from the store is already fully cooked, so why would you need a special instant pot recipe? Sometimes adding spices to your ham can enhance the flavor, plus for a special occasion you want it warmed up. Ham makes a great Christmas alternative to turkey or prime rib.

SERVES: Four or more

PREPARATION TIME: 15 minutes

INGREDIENTS:

- 1 cup light brown sugar

- 2 tablespoons water or cider vinegar

- ½ teaspoon cloves, ground

INSTRUCTIONS:

1. Heat the water.

2. Add in the light brown sugar and use the water to melt it.

3. Add in the cloves.

4. Using a pastry brush, spread the glaze over the ham edges.

5. Place the entire ham in the instant pot.

6. Heat for 5 minutes.

ADDITIONAL SUGGESTIONS:

The vinegar will give the glaze a little kick to tamp down the sweetness. You can also forgo the vinegar if you like a sweeter ham. If you like ham really sweet, consider using a little pineapple juice in place of the water or vinegar. You can also put some pineapple chunks in with the ham to enhance the flavor. Serve the ham with side dishes such as mashed potatoes, macaroni with five cheeses, green beans, biscuits, or other favorite side dishes.

**Prime Rib**

Prime rib is definitely prime because of its tender cut. It makes a wonderful Christmas or special occasion entrée to go with your other favorites. The key is to ensure it is cooked to your "doneness" level, without drying out the meat.

SERVES: Two or more

PREPARATION TIME: 1 hour

INGREDIENTS:

- Two bone rib roast (one bone for each person)

- Butter

- Salt

- Pepper

- 1 cup water

- Other seasonings

- Carrots

- Potatoes

INSTRUCTIONS:

1. Cut up any vegetables you are going to cook with your roast.

2. Using a little oil in the pot of the instant pot, set it to sauté.

3. Brown the outside of the prime rib, with a little butter, salt and pepper to taste.

4. Add additional seasonings if you prefer.

5. Use the trivet.

6.  Place 1 cup water in the bottom of the instant pot.

7.  Carrots and potatoes do take time, but you do not want to overcook them either. Set the veggies aside for now.

8.  Put the roast in the instant pot.

9.  Set the timer for 15 minutes.

10. Use the quick release button to release the steam.

11. Add in the veggies.

12. Set the timer for another 15 minutes.

13. Check the roast. If you like a rare roast, the temperature should be 130 degrees F. At 140 to 145 degrees F the roast will be medium rare. You may need to add to the cooking time to get the roast done to the proper temperature for you.

ADDITIONAL SUGGESTIONS:

Prime rib is perfect with mashed potatoes, carrots, green beans, and a muffin or roll. You can add a variety of seasonings for the taste you prefer or go with a simple salt and pepper flavor allowing the meat to speak for itself.

## Instant Pot Lasagna

Lasagna is a classic dish that is often served at weddings and special occasions. If you don't have the time to make one in the oven, then consider preparing one in your instant pot to shave some time off the actual baking process.

SERVES: Four

PREPARATION TIME: 1 hour

INGREDIENTS:

- 1 16-ounce package ricotta cheese

- 16 ounces shredded mozzarella

- ½ cup Parmesan cheese, grated

- ½ tablespoon black pepper

- ½ tablespoon garlic powder

- ½ pound Italian sausage or hamburger meat

- 3 tablespoons olive oil

- ¼ cup basil

- 1 16-ounce jar pasta sauce

- 1 box oven ready noodles

INSTRUCTIONS:

1. Grab a pan that is going to fit in your instant pot. It should be a deep dish to make enough pasta for everyone.

2. Use the oil to grease the pan.

3. If using uncooked meat, make sure you cook it first.

4. Using alternative layers, start with pasta sauce, noodles, cheeses, meat, and sauce.

5. Build the layers until you run out of noodles.

6. Make sure you top the layers with more ricotta, sauce, meat, and cheese.

7. Cover the pan with aluminum foil.

8. Use the trivet.

9. Place 1.5 cups of water in the pot of the pot.

10. Cook on high pressure for 20 minutes.

11. Let the steam release naturally for 20 minutes.

12. Serve.

ADDITIONAL SUGGESTIONS:

You can always change the ingredients of a lasagna, such as adding in spinach to enhance the health benefits of your meal. Serve with garlic bread, a salad, or soup.

# Chapter 9: Two Person Meals

Any of the meals in this chapter can be expanded for more people. They are dinner or lunch recipes, simply created for a two-person meal requirement. You will discover they have all the nutrients you need for a healthy meal. Also, many of the recipes in this book can be adapted for two people. It is a matter of changing the amounts of ingredients to fit your needs.

## Adobo Pork

Adobo is a staple food in southeast Asia and Latin America. This recipe is a Latin American adobo. You can enhance the healthy quality of this dish by using fresh herbs and spices instead of the ones already dried and placed in a container for you. Ancho chilies are poblano chilies, which may help you find them in the store. Their flavor is extremely rich compared to other chilies.

SERVES: Two

PREPARATION TIME: approximately 40 minutes

INGREDIENTS:

- 2 pork chops

- 1 cup and 2 tablespoons chicken or vegetable broth

- 1 cup Arborio rice

- 2 ancho chilies, seeded, de-stemmed, chopped

- ½ teaspoon cumin, ground

- ¼ onion, chopped

- ½ teaspoon dried oregano

- ½ teaspoon black pepper

- ¼ teaspoon ground allspice

- 2 tablespoons cider vinegar

- 2 teaspoons lime juice, from a fresh lime

- 4 tablespoons orange juice

- 1 green pepper, cut into even strips

INSTRUCTIONS:

1. Set your instant pot up to sauté your pork chops for 5 minutes, use a little oil.

2. Add remainder of the ingredients to the pot, except for the rice.

3. Cancel sauté and select meat.

4. Set time to 25 minutes.

5. Make sure your valve is sealing correctly.

6. Let it stand for 10 minutes after it is done.

7. In the meantime, get out your rice cooker.

8. Place enough water in the rice cooker for the cup of rice you are going to cook.

9. The rice will take 25 minutes, with it standing for an additional 5 minutes to finish.

10. Serve the pork over the rice.

ADDITIONAL SUGGESTIONS:

If you like mild spice use Anaheim chilies, which are a milder Chile than ancho. You can also use pork butt or shoulder cut for this recipe. You will want to cut these larger meats into large cubes.

**African Peanut Butter Stew**

African Peanut Butter Stew is a popular dish from Gabon, Africa. It is also a staple meal on many tables in the USA and Europe as its popularity grows. Use fresh ingredients to keep the taste.

SERVES: Two

PREPARATION TIME: 30 minutes

INGREDIENTS:

- 2 pieces of chicken breast

- ½ onion, diced

- ¾ cup rice

- ½ orange bell pepper

- ¾ cup and 1 tablespoon water or chicken broth

- 2/3 cup water or milk

- 2 crushed or minced garlic cloves

- ½ teaspoon cayenne pepper

- 3 tablespoons peanut butter

- 3 tomatoes

- 1 handful spinach leaves

- 1 carrot, diced

INSTRUCTIONS:

1. Use a rice cooker to cook your rice.

2. Prep your instant pot to cook chicken.

3. Dice your vegetables.

4. Add all, but the peanut butter into your instant pot.

5. Cook for 15 minutes, to cook the chicken thoroughly.

6. Stir in the peanut butter at the end.

ADDITIONAL SUGGESTIONS:

You can add more peanut butter and adjust the seasonings to taste if you wish. Consider topping your meal with peanuts for garnish. Also, consider using noodles, such as Soba versus rice.

**Pasta with Shellfish**

Shellfish provides omega fatty acids that are helpful to your health. If you like shellfish, this is a great way to have a quick meal for dinner. You have several options for how to incorporate the shellfish, such as pasta filled with a fish concoction or simply creating a pasta and fish dish, where the shellfish is served over the top.

SERVES: Two

PREPARATION TIME: 20 minutes, approximately

INGREDIENTS:

- 1 cups pasta (penne, farfalle)

- 1/3 cup plus 1 tablespoon water

- 3 drops olive oil

- ½ onion, finely chopped

- 4 minced garlic cloves

- ½ pound seafood, fresh or frozen

- 1 cups spinach, fresh and washed

- 4 Roma tomatoes, thickly sliced

INSTRUCTIONS:

1. Start by adding the water and pasta to the instant pot.

2. Cook for 5 minutes.

3. Open the instant pot, being careful of the steam.

4. Add in the olive oil, garlic, onion, seafood, spinach, and tomatoes

5. Cook for an additional 5 minutes, if the seafood is frozen.

ADDITIONAL SUGGESTIONS:

When using thawed shellfish, you may need to adapt the times. Mussels take 2 to 3 minutes to cook in an instant pot, while shrimp or prawns only take 1 to 2 minutes. The pasta is still going to take 10 minutes' total, so you want to make certain you are not stopping the pasta too early or overcooking the shellfish.

**Beef Brisket**

SERVES: Two

PREPARATION TIME: 1 ½ hours

INGREDIENTS:

- 2-pounds brisket meat, such as flank steak

- 32-ounces beef broth or water

- 3 gloves of garlic, minced

- ½ large onion, sliced as thin as possible

- Black pepper to taste

- 3 large carrots

- Barbecue sauce or teriyaki sauce (optional)

INSTRUCTIONS:

1. Using a healthy oil, such as coconut or avocado oil, coat the bottom of your instant pot.

2. Turn on sauté and brown the brisket and onions.

3. Browning should take 7 minutes per side.

4. Make sure the onions are underneath the meat.

5. Pour in the beef broth, dump in the carrots and garlic.

6. Set the timer for 50 minutes.

7. Check the meat.

8. If tender, serve.

ADDITIONAL SUGGESTIONS:

You can make your own barbecue or teriyaki sauce. You can also use the broth from the instant pot to create a gravy, if you prefer.

**Chicken Fajitas**

Fajitas are a great, quick meal, with plenty of nutrients from the peppers and onions. If you need to walk away from the kitchen while your dinner is being cooked, this is a wonderful instant pot recipe to use.

SERVES: Two

PREPARATION TIME: 20 minutes, approximately

INGREDIENTS:

- 1-pound chicken

- 1 each: green, yellow, red, and orange pepper

- 1 large onion

- Chili powder

- Pepper

- 1 garlic clove, minced

- ¼ cup water

INSTRUCTIONS:

1. Slice all the veggies into thin strips.

2. Make your chicken about the same size as the veggie strips.

3. Mix the chili powder, pepper, garlic and water.

4. Place the seasoning mixture in the instant pot.

5. Add in the veggies and chicken.

6. Cook for 10 minutes.

7. Let steam stand for 5 minutes.

8. Check the temperature of the chicken. The chicken should be 165 degrees F, internally.

9. Warm tortilla shells using the steam basket and steam function on the instant pot, about 30 seconds.

10. Place the tortilla shells on a plate, fill with the drained chicken mixture, and top with a Mexican cheese blend.

11. Serve with sour cream and guacamole.

ADDITIONAL SUGGESTIONS:

For side dishes, consider refried beans, Mexican

# Chapter 10: Additional Suggestions:

The Instant Pot can save time for you. As you looked through the various recipes in the above chapters you should have noticed that numerous recipes used less time to cook a full meal than what you are used to.

An Instant Pot is naturally going to save you time in a variety of ways:

- Clean up takes less time since you have less to clean.

- The high pressure and temperatures help you cook the meal evenly and in less time.

But, what about the preparation? Are there ways to save time on preparing all the meats, veggies, and other foods you are going to include in your meal?

Yes. There are some tips that can be provided to help you reduce the time it takes for you to make a meal based on the preparation time alone. The cooking time is already reduced, so let's discover how you can save more time in the kitchen.

1. The day you shop expect to spend an hour in the kitchen with all the fresh foods you purchased.

2. Cut up all the veggies into the appropriate size and slices for the recipes you are going to use for that week.

3. Store the veggies in a little water to keep them moist.

4. Use containers and label them based on the menu item you are going to create with them.

Mason Jar meals have become extremely popular because you can simply grab a mason jar and eat, if it is a salad or pasta salad. The same concept can be applied to your recipes for the week.

Have a container of all the veggies you need for one recipe, except for the meat. The meat should be kept out of the veggie container because it is raw. However, you can also put the amount of meat you need for the recipe in a container or bag, labeled, so you can grab it and the cut-up veggies and put everything in the Instant Pot.

Use the delay setting. When you get up in the morning and need to make dinner, put everything in the pot and set the delay. It can be cooking when you arrive home to eat.

Have a second insert, so you can cook at least two meals without needing to clean up first. For example, if you make breakfast, then you can have a pot to insert for your dinner meal. After you eat dinner you can clean both pots.

These are just a few of the ways you can save time in your preparations, as well as in the process of making your meals. As you get used to your Instant Pot, you may find other ways to save your time. The important factor is that you save time by using a one-pot cooker versus coming home and making an elaborate meal using the stove and oven.

# Conclusion

I hope you have gained a lot from this book. Thank you for your purchase. The Instant Pot is a great device that will make your life simpler, once you take the plunge and make your purchase. If you already have an Instant Pot, hopefully you have gained some insight into how to use it, the functions it offers, and new recipes to try.

The recipes included may be simple, but they are enough to get you started. You now have a guide to see how some of the most popular, tasty recipes can be turned into Instant Pot meals. Whether you decide to cook rice with the meal or use the rice cooker feature before you cook the rest of your meal, you know you have a device that will serve all of your purposes. You can also cook a pot roast that will have your taste buds dancing happy all night.

The Instant Pot makes cooking under pressure safe; especially, if you have little children in your home.

Let this multifunctional pot save you on your energy bill, water bill, and time. Plenty of time can be saved when you are cooking everything all at once instead of using multiple pots and having to clean up the mess that comes from such an elaborate meal.

CPSIA information can be obtained
at www.ICGtesting.com
Printed in the USA
LVOW13s1549160217

524503LV00009B/770/P

9 781540 783158